DANIEL

REFORMED EXPOSITORY BIBLE STUDIES

A Companion Series to the Reformed Expository Commentaries

Series Editors

Daniel M. Doriani
Iain M. Duguid
Richard D. Phillips
Philip Graham Ryken

Daniel: Faith Enduring through Adversity
Galatians: The Gospel of Free Grace
James: Portrait of a Living Faith

DANIEL

FAITH ENDURING THROUGH ADVERSITY

A 13-LESSON STUDY

REFORMED EXPOSITORY
BIBLE STUDY

JON NIELSON

P&R

PUBLISHING

P.O. BOX 817 • PHILLIPSBURG • NEW JERSEY 08865-0817

ISBN: 978-1-62995-679-4 (pbk)
ISBN: 978-1-62995-680-0 (ePub)
ISBN: 978-1-62995-681-7 (Mobi)

Printed in the United States of America

CONTENTS

SERIES INTRODUCTION

Studying the Bible will change your life. This is the consistent witness of Scripture and the experience of people all over the world, in every period of church history.

King David said, "The law of the LORD is perfect, reviving the soul; the testimony of the LORD is sure, making wise the simple; the precepts of the LORD are right, rejoicing the heart; the commandment of the LORD is pure, enlightening the eyes" (Ps. 19:7–8). So anyone who wants to be wiser and happier, and who wants to feel more alive, with a clearer perception of spiritual reality, should study the Scriptures.

Whether we study the Bible alone or with other Christians, it will change us from the inside out. The Reformed Expository Bible Studies provide tools for biblical transformation. Written as a companion to the Reformed Expository Commentary, this series of short books for personal or group study is designed to help people study the Bible for themselves, understand its message, and then apply its truths to daily life.

Each Bible study is introduced by a pastor-scholar who has written a full-length expository commentary on the same book of the Bible. The individual chapters start with the summary of a Bible passage, explaining **The Big Picture** of this portion of God's Word. Then the questions in **Getting Started** introduce one or two of the passage's main themes in ways that connect to life experience. These questions may be especially helpful for group leaders in generating lively conversation.

Understanding the Bible's message starts with seeing what is actually there, which is where **Observing the Text** comes in. Then the Bible study provides a longer and more in-depth set of questions entitled **Understanding the Text**. These questions carefully guide students through the entire passage, verse by verse or section by section.

It is important not to read a Bible passage in isolation, but to see it in the wider context of Scripture. So each Bible study includes two **Bible Connections** questions that invite readers to investigate passages from other places in Scripture—passages that add important background, offer valuable contrasts or comparisons, and especially connect the main passage to the person and work of Jesus Christ.

The next section is one of the most distinctive features of the Reformed Expository Bible Studies. The authors believe that the Bible teaches important doctrines of the Christian faith, and that reading biblical literature is enhanced when we know something about its underlying theology. The questions in **Theology Connections** identify some of these doctrines by bringing the Bible passage into conversation with creeds and confessions from the Reformed tradition, as well as with learned theologians of the church.

Our aim in all of this is to help ordinary Christians apply biblical truth to daily life. **Applying the Text** uses open-ended questions to get people thinking about sins that need to be confessed, attitudes that need to change, and areas of new obedience that need to come alive by the power and influence of the Holy Spirit. Finally, each study ends with a **Prayer Prompt** that invites Bible students to respond to what they are learning with petitions for God's help and words of praise and gratitude.

You will notice boxed quotations throughout the Bible study. These quotations come from one of the volumes in the Reformed Expository Commentary. Although the Bible study can stand alone and includes everything you need for a life-changing encounter with a book of the Bible, it is also intended to serve as a companion to a full commentary on the same biblical book. Reading the full commentary is especially useful for teachers who want to help their students answer the questions in the Bible study at a deeper level, as well as for students who wish to further enrich their own biblical understanding.

The people who worked together to produce this series of Bible studies have prayed that they will engage you more intimately with Scripture, producing the kind of spiritual transformation that only the Bible can bring.

Philip Graham Ryken
Coeditor of the Reformed Expository Commentary series

INTRODUCING DANIEL

The book of Daniel records the life and visions of the man of the same name, a Judean born into a noble family during the latter part of the seventh century B.C. He was taken into exile in Babylon by Nebuchadnezzar in 605 B.C., while still a young man, and spent his whole life in exile, though he did live long enough to see the promised return of the exiles to Judah begin to take place in the days of Cyrus, almost seventy years later (Dan. 6:28). During his lifetime, many of his fellow countrymen joined him in exile in Babylon, especially after the fall of Jerusalem in 586 B.C. The book's **main purpose** is to encourage believers to live as strangers and exiles in a world that is not their home and never will be (cf. 1 Peter 2:11), while at the same time seeking the *shalom* (well-being) of the city, town, or village in which God has providentially placed them (cf. Jer. 29:7). The book has a particular resonance for believers who are being violently persecuted for their faith.

There is no explicit claim to **authorship** within the book. The opening narratives about Daniel and his friends, Shadrach, Meshach, and Abednego, are in the third person, as is the introduction to the apocalyptic visions in Daniel 7:1. The visions themselves are in the first person, recounted by Daniel himself. It is customary in scholarly circles to assume a late date (and therefore **audience**) for the book, somewhere during the reign of Antiochus IV Epiphanes (175–164 B.C.), since the apocalyptic visions include precise predictions of numerous well-attested historical events between Daniel's own day and the mid-second century. This later date was also a time of great persecution for the Jewish community, when the writings of Daniel would undoubtedly have found a fresh relevance among God's persecuted people.

Because of the accuracy and specificity of these predictions, many scholars assume that they must have been made after the events that they describe. But if God is truly sovereign over history, then it makes sense that he would demonstrate that reality by means of genuinely predictive prophecy, such as is found in Daniel 8–11 (see Isa. 44:6–8; 46:8–11). The Lord's claim to be able to predict the future would remain empty if he never followed through and demonstrated the truth of his claim through fulfilled prophecy. The fact that the Lord is able to predict the future in such detail testifies to his sovereign control over all of history, in exactly the same way that his remarkable deliverances of Daniel and his friends do. This demonstration of the Lord's existence and power would have been intensely relevant to a Jewish audience in the sixth century B.C. Living in exile in Babylon, they would have been continually bombarded by propaganda for Marduk and the other false gods of the Babylonians, especially after Jerusalem's fall to the Babylonian army. Even though Daniel's hearers would not themselves live to see the fulfillment of those prophecies, the very existence of them would have strengthened their faith in the reality and power of Israel's God. How much more should they serve to encourage believers today, who can see their exact fulfillment!

Other reasons have also been advanced for assigning a late date to the book, such as the presence of Persian and Greek loan words in it. However, given the widespread trade connections of Babylon at its height, there is no reason why such words could not have been in currency in Daniel's day (if indeed they are from these languages, and not separately derived from other sources). It is true that there remain some historical conundrums in the book to which we do not yet have definitive answers, such as the identity of Darius and his relationship to Cyrus. But our knowledge of this time period is far from complete, and other alleged discrepancies have been resolved. For example, until recently, it was claimed that Belshazzar could not have been a real person as described by Daniel: we have a complete list of Babylonian kings, and the king reigning when Babylon fell to the Persians was Nabonidus. However, more recent archaeological studies have uncovered references to "Bel-Shar-Utsur," the son of Nabonidus, who was co-regent with him for part of his reign, governing Babylon during his lengthy absences from the capital. It is not clear how a writer composing a *de novo* account in the second century B.C. would have even known Belshazzar's name. There is therefore no solid reason to believe that the book was composed long after Daniel's time, or that it does not accurately record Daniel's own experiences and apocalyptic visions.

As for its **structure and themes**, the book of Daniel divides into two parts in terms of genre. The opening narrative, chapters 1–6, explores models of how Daniel's Jewish compatriots might live faithfully in exile, seeking the *shalom* of the city where God had placed them (see Jer. 29), while resisting the pressure to assimilate to Babylonian culture and religion. These stories would have provided immediate help to the exiles, as well as guidance for generations of believers since then, for the normal mode of existence of God's people in this world is as sojourners and exiles in an often hostile environment. The book of Daniel assures the Lord's people that he is with them, even in the most difficult and painful experiences of life (Dan. 3:24–25). The Lord is able to protect them against their pagan oppressors if he so chooses, but even if not, faithfulness to him is more precious than life itself (Dan. 3:17–18). The book also shows proud and boastful Nebuchadnezzar being humbled by God, before finally being restored to his former position, now with a new appreciation of God's existence and power (Dan. 4). God is the one who raises up and brings down kings and empires, no matter how boastful their claims about themselves may be. History records a continual succession of such empires, which come and go without leaving a lasting legacy. Meanwhile, God is building his own kingdom, which is a kingdom without end.

The latter portion of the book, chapters 7–12, is written in apocalyptic form. These dramatic visions have a message that dovetails with the themes of chapters 1–6. They provided encouragement and hope to the marginalized exiles, reminding them that it is the Ancient of Days who is the judge of the living and the dead, not the Babylonians (Dan. 7:9–10). A succession of world empires would become ever more frightening and menacing toward God's people, but the Lord would rule sovereignly over all the complex struggles of world history, and he would ultimately give the verdict on behalf of his saints (7:18). The times and seasons are in his hand, and the sufferings of his people are carefully measured out and limited by him. Apocalyptic literature uncovers for us the heavenly reality that stands behind the affairs of men and nations that we can see with our eyes—a heavenly reality to which we are mostly blind. It lifts the curtain and shows us the truth of the sovereign reign of our God in glorious color. It also reminds us that this present age of conflict and suffering for God's people will soon be replaced by another age, an eschatological age of peace. It is worth remaining faithful to God in the meantime, therefore, no matter what the cost to us may be—even if it costs us our very lives—because the eternal future belongs to our God and to his faithful ones.

Part of the book of Daniel is written in the international diplomatic language of Aramaic, rather than Hebrew (Dan. 2:4–7:28), perhaps because these chapters deal with more universal concerns, rather than simply Israelite matters. That feature binds together the narrative and apocalyptic portions and highlights the chiastic structure of chapters 2–7 (see below). At their heart, the two halves of the book have essentially the same message, which spoke to essentially the same audience of exiles, and speaks as well to all of us as their heirs: stand firm in the midst of the fiery furnace of life, for the Lord is with his people in their sufferings, and he will ultimately bring them through many trials to a joyful end.

OUTLINE

1. Narrative (1:1–6:28)
   A. Prologue: Daniel and friends taken into exile and resisting assimilation (1:1–21)
   B. Nebuchadnezzar's dream of a great statue (2:1–49)
   C. Nebuchadnezzar builds a great statue (3:1–30)
   D. Nebuchadnezzar brought low and restored (4:1–37)
   E. Belshazzar's feast (5:1–31)
   F. Daniel in the lion's den (6:1–28)
2. Apocalyptic (7:1–12:13)
   A. First vision: four terrifying beasts and the Ancient of Days (7:1–28)
   B. Second vision: the ram, the goat, and the little horn (8:1–27)
   C. Daniel's prayer and its answer: the seventy weeks (9:1–27)
   D. Third vision: wars and rumors of wars until the time of the end (10:1–12:13)

CHIASTIC ARRANGEMENT OF THE ARAMAIC SECTION

A. Four earthly kingdoms and the kingdom of God (2:4–49)
  B. God delivers his servants: Shadrach, Meshach, and
     Abednego (3:1–30)
     C. Nebuchadnezzar humbled and restored (4:1–37)
     C. Belshazzar humbled and destroyed (5:1–31)
  B. God delivers his servants: Daniel (6:1–28)
A. Four earthly kingdoms and the kingdom of God (7:1–28)

Iain M. Duguid
Coeditor of the Reformed Expository Commentary series
Author of *Daniel* (REC)

LESSON 1

WHEN THE WORLD
DOES ITS WORST

Daniel 1:1–21

THE BIG PICTURE

The book of Daniel begins at a very sad point in the history of Israel: the fall of Jerusalem to Nebuchadnezzar, king of Babylon, and the exile of many of the people of Judah to Babylon. This exile comes as God's judgment against his sinful people—a judgment that he has warned them about through the messages of his prophets many times. As part of Babylon's victory, Nebuchadnezzar commissions a certain group of gifted and attractive young Israelite men to take part in a special program in Babylon. Daniel, along with three of his friends, is chosen to be part of this group—probably best understood as a kind of reprogramming enterprise to turn some of the best young Israelites into fully adapted Babylonians. In the passage you will study today, though, you will see Daniel and his friends clinging to their identity as people of the Lord, even in the midst of exile. We will read of God's faithfulness to these brave and faith-filled young men as he grants them great favor and success. Because of God's grace, even as Daniel and his friends reject the foods and practices of Babylon, they rise to the top of the ranks of those around them. God's faithful plans for his people will continue—even during the years of exile.

Read Daniel 1:1–21.

GETTING STARTED

1. Have you ever lived for a time in a culture that was unfamiliar to you—or perhaps only visited such a place? If so, what struggles and frustrations did you face? In what ways did you feel pressure to assimilate to the surrounding culture?

2. What beliefs or practices as a follower of Jesus Christ have caused you to feel most out of step with your local culture and social circle? In what areas of your life have you run into conflict, social marginalization, or ridicule because of your commitment to God and his Word?

God's Presence in Judgment, pg. 7

The recognition that their fate came from the hand of God as a faithful act of judgment was itself an encouragement to the exiles. Their future was not controlled by Babylon or its gods, but by the Lord, the God of heaven (Dan. 2:19). The one who had sent them into exile had also promised to be with them there, and ultimately to restore them from exile after a time of judgment.

OBSERVING THE TEXT

3. What do you notice about the narrator's mention of God's role in the defeat and exile of his people (1:2)? How might this be an important verse for setting the stage for the entire book? What theological truths are communicated here?

4. How does the narrator talk about the role of God throughout the rest of the narrative? In what ways is God active in this account?

5. While the narrator does not give details about the internal monologue or inner thoughts of Daniel and his friends, their actions certainly tell us much about who they are. What are some ways in which you would describe Daniel and the other young men, based on your initial reading of this passage?

UNDERSTANDING THE TEXT

6. Looking at Daniel 1:3–5, and particularly the specific commands of King Nebuchadnezzar, what seems to be his motivation in this special

program for some of the Israelite young men? What might he be seeking to accomplish over the course of three years?

7. What is significant about the changing of the names of Daniel, Hananiah, Mishael, and Azariah (1:6–7)? What might the chief official in Babylon be seeking to signal to these young men?

8. Why might Daniel and his friends have refused to eat the royal food and wine that was supplied to them (1:8)? Daniel 10:3 indicates that Daniel did not permanently abstain from Babylonian food. What might these Israelite men have been communicating to the Babylonians—and perhaps to themselves as well—through their abstention?

9. Why is the result of the test (1:15–16) surprising, in human terms? How is this evidence of God's hidden and faithful hand in caring for Daniel and his friends?

Whose Faithfulness?, pg. 14
The focus throughout this chapter is not simply the faithfulness of these four young men to their God, however. It is on God's faithfulness to them. It was God who cause them to find mercy . . . in the eyes of their captors. . . . This outcome too was a mark of God's faithfulness to these young men, honoring their commitment to him.

10. What does 1:17 reveal more explicitly about God's hand in this period of dieting and testing? What other special capacities and success does God grant to these young men? What does all of this teach us about God's character and his devotion to his people?

11. Daniel 1:21 briefly looks seventy years into the future, mentioning that Daniel will remain in Babylon until the beginning of the reign of King Cyrus. Why might the narrator have included that detail here in the book? How might this connect to the truths about God to which this chapter has been pointing?

BIBLE CONNECTIONS

12. As you may know, the exile of God's people did not come as a complete surprise. Take a moment to glance back at Leviticus 26:14–39 (note especially verses 33 and 39). How had God warned his people about unrepentant sin, hundreds of years before the time of Daniel? What did God say with regard to exile?

13. Toward the end of his reign, King Hezekiah made the terrible mistake of showing off the treasures of his house to a group of envoys

from Babylon. Read 2 Kings 20:16–18. What is the prophecy against Hezekiah that results from his actions? What can you conclude about his motivation for what he did, and why might God have reacted so strongly?

THEOLOGY CONNECTIONS

14. In describing Christ's purpose for the church, the authors of the Westminster Confession of Faith write: "Unto this catholic visible church Christ hath given the ministry, oracles, and ordinances of God, for the gathering and perfecting of the saints, in this life, to the end of the world: and doth, by his own presence and Spirit, according to his promise, make them effectual thereunto" (25.3). According to this affirmation, how might the church have a role in strengthening Christians who live in spiritual "exile" while on earth? In what ways can the church strengthen its sense of identity as God's people in the midst of a hostile culture?

15. For centuries, faithful Christians have sought to balance the commitment to remaining *undefiled* by the world with efforts to *engage* the world and its culture for the sake of the gospel of Jesus Christ. Extreme commitments to the former have sometimes resulted in separatist movements of various kinds, while some Christians have abandoned the uniqueness of the gospel in their efforts to connect with culture. Can

you point to any biblical or theological principles that might help us maintain the balance between these two extremes?

APPLYING THE TEXT

16. As we consider the reprogramming efforts of the Babylonian king and his officials, exerted on Daniel and his friends, how might we better discern the pressures and assimilative efforts of our culture today? What strategies might the Enemy use to draw us away from our identity in Christ and as people of God's Word?

17. What can we, as spiritual exiles in this world, learn from the behavior of the young men in the first chapter of Daniel? What do they refuse, and why is this important? In what do they fully participate, and how can we apply this to our engagement with our culture?

Deliverance for the Compromised, pg. 16
The good news of the gospel, however, is not simply that God is faithful to those who are faithful to him. It is that a Savior has come to deliver faithless and compromised saints like us. Our salvation rests not on our ability to remain undefiled by the world, but rather on the pure and undefiled offering that Jesus has provided in our place.

18. How must participation, service, and worship in the context of the local church serve to reinforce our ultimate identity, belonging, and citizenship? In what ways can the proclamation of the gospel in our churches remind us that we are exiles and that our foremost allegiance is to Jesus Christ?

PRAYER PROMPT

As you close this first lesson in Daniel with prayer, consider your role as an "elect exile" in this world through faith in Jesus Christ (1 Peter 1:1). Like Daniel, you live in the midst of a fallen world, undergoing almost constant assaults on your faith. Ask God for strength to hold on to your identity in Christ, as you cling to his Word and link arms with his people. Thank him for a perfect and undefiled Savior who graciously saves defiled sinners like us, and pray that he would give you courage and strength to stand for him.

LESSON 2

INTERESTING TIMES

Daniel 2:1–23

THE BIG PICTURE

Between Daniel chapters 1 and 2, Daniel has presumably continued to work and serve faithfully during the time of exile in Babylon. He is a young man with dual identities, as he clings to his faith in the Lord and his Word, while also serving in support of the kingdom of King Nebuchadnezzar. Daniel 2, however, describes a day in Daniel's life—probably unanticipated by him—in which he was suddenly yanked into the spotlight of the entire empire. The king of Babylon is in emotional turmoil, having had a deeply unsettling dream that he cannot interpret. In a fit of unreasonable rage, he demands that his counselors not only interpret the dream for him, but also tell him the contents of it—which are known only to him. With their lives hanging in the balance, these royal viziers turn to Daniel and his Hebrew friends. Our passage for this lesson shows these young men of faith seeking "mercy from the God of heaven" (v. 18), who graciously answers their prayers by revealing both the substance and the meaning of King Nebuchadnezzar's dream. As Daniel responds with a prayer of praise to God (2:20–23), we begin to see the triumph of God's wisdom over the wisdom of Babylon—a theme that will continue in the next part of the chapter.

Read Daniel 2:1–23.

GETTING STARTED

1. Most of the days of our lives are relatively ordinary; even people with fascinating jobs experience mundane moments and daily routines. As you consider your life, what would you identify as some of its most exciting moments or seasons? What have been some of the most disturbing or challenging times of your life?

2. Have you ever been forced into an important position or a key opportunity in a completely unexpected way? How did you respond? In what ways did you seek to see God's hand in that situation, and how did you elicit his help and strength?

The Times That Stand Out, pg. 18
The times in Daniel's life that Scripture records for us are the "interesting times"—the moments when Daniel's two loyalties clashed sharply with each other, or when his life was threatened in some way or another. . . . At these special times of stress and trial, it was made evident to all those around Daniel that the Lord was working in and through his life in a special way.

OBSERVING THE TEXT

3. Based on your initial reading of this passage, what do you notice about the behavior and character of King Nebuchadnezzar? How would you describe his personality, his words, and his actions?

4. Given what you know from your study of Scripture (and perhaps some knowledge of ancient culture), why might the interpretation of this dream have been so important to the king? What significance is attached to dreams throughout the Bible? How does God use them?

5. What do you notice about Daniel's prayer of thanksgiving to God, which concludes the passage for this lesson? What themes are central to this prayer, and what does Daniel affirm about God's ways and his character?

UNDERSTANDING THE TEXT

6. What is predictable in the opening verses of this chapter (2:1–4)? What is surprising about the king's demand to his astrologers (2:5–6)? How do they respond to it?

7. Why is the king's demand so beyond the capabilities of the wise men, according to their own words in 2:10–11? Who would be able to meet such a request? How might the narrator be using their words to set up the events that will follow, involving both Daniel and God?

8. What does Daniel's response to the demand of the king reveal about his character and faith in God (2:17–19)? How is his response a model of humility and reliance upon the grace and mercy of God? In what ways does Daniel involve his friends in his seeking help from God?

9. What is significant about the *content* of Daniel's prayer of thanksgiving (2:20–23)? What is significant about its *timing*? What attributes and actions of God does Daniel seem to celebrate the most?

The Uniqueness of God, pg. 21
Thus in [the wise men's] view what the king asked of them was something impossible for human wisdom to accomplish. Here we see the uniqueness of the God of the Bible, who is both able and willing to reveal his plans and purposes to mankind.

10. What, specifically, is this passage teaching us about the power and ways of God—both in the events of the narrative and in the words and prayer of Daniel?

11. How does this passage show the contrast between the wisdom of the world (Babylon) and the wisdom of God? How is worldly wisdom deficient in this passage? How might this battle for true wisdom point us to Jesus Christ and the gospel?

BIBLE CONNECTIONS

12. As you may remember, God has used the special gift of his wisdom to bring his people favor with pagan rulers before. Scan through Genesis 40, and note Joseph's elevation before Pharaoh because of the God-given interpretation of his dreams. How did this bring glory to God? How did God ultimately use the elevation of Joseph to leadership in Egypt?

13. The apostle John, in the well-known prologue to his gospel, tells of the wonders of the eternal Word of God becoming flesh to dwell among us. Take a minute to read through John 1:1–14. What does John tell us about the coming of Jesus, the eternal "logos" (Word) of God? How

does the life and work of Jesus Christ reveal the full wisdom of God to his world?

THEOLOGY CONNECTIONS

14. Considering God's definition of "wisdom," as revealed in the Old Testament, the great Reformer Martin Luther once wrote: "In turn Solomon calls folly all that which proceeds without God's word and works. A wise man, then, is one who guides himself by God's word and works; a fool is one who presumptuously guides himself by his own mind and notions."[1] How might these truths about God's wisdom and his Word be deduced from a study of Daniel 2:1–23?

15. The Heidelberg Catechism describes the work of Jesus, in part, by explaining that he "fully reveals to us the secret counsel and will of God concerning our deliverance" (Q&A 31). Given this reality about the revelatory work of Jesus, how might we understand this passage from Daniel 2 as foreshadowing the work of Christ explicitly?

1. Martin Luther, "Preface to the Proverbs of Solomon" (1524), in *Luther's Works*, vol. 35, *Word and Sacrament I*, ed. E. Theodore Bachmann and Helmut T. Lehmann (Philadelphia: Muhlenberg Press, 1960), 262.

APPLYING THE TEXT

16. As you consider Daniel's response to this seemingly insurmountable challenge, how might you learn from his model of prayer, humility, and seeking mercy from God? How could his approach serve as a model for your prayer and seeking God in difficult times?

17. In what ways should this passage strengthen your confidence in the wisdom of God, revealed most fully in Jesus Christ and his gospel, as opposed to the supposed wisdom of the world?

18. Of what aspects of God's character, and his ways of working in the world, does this passage remind you? How ought this passage to encourage you as you seek to faithfully live daily for God?

God's Glory Revealed, pg. 28

This part of the Book of Daniel points us forward to Christ. In Christ, God definitively came to live among men, thereby disproving once for all the theology of the Babylonian diviners that the gods do not dwell among men. . . . In Christ, God became flesh and made his dwelling among us. In him, we saw revealed the glory of the one and only true God.

PRAYER PROMPT

As you conclude this study of Daniel 2:1–23 and approach God in prayer, be encouraged that you serve the all-wise King of the universe. His wisdom far surpasses the wisdom of the world; he reveals and conceals as he pleases. In prayer, ask him for strength to humbly seek him in the midst of troubles. Pray that he would strengthen you in an unshakeable faith in his Son, in whom are hidden "all the treasures of wisdom and knowledge" (Col. 2:3).

LESSON 3

GONE WITH THE WIND
Daniel 2:24–49

THE BIG PICTURE

As you began your study of Daniel 2 in the last lesson, you saw King Nebuchadnezzar forcing the wise men of Babylon (including Daniel!) into a dangerous situation. He had demanded the impossible, following an unsettling dream: provide the contents of the dream, along with its interpretation, or face execution. God, in his grace, provided the interpretation to Daniel, revealing his wisdom, which far surpassed the greatest wisdom of Babylon. Now, in the second part of Daniel 2, we read of Daniel's interaction with King Nebuchadnezzar, his summary and interpretation of the king's dream, and the king's enthusiastic response to Daniel—both in praising his God and in exalting Daniel and his friends to even higher positions in Babylon. True to his character, Daniel deflects credit and gives glory to God, who through King Nebuchadnezzar's dream is revealing the coming glory of the kingdom of his Son. This coming kingdom will be eternal—far surpassing the transient empires of this world.

Read Daniel 2:24–49.

GETTING STARTED

1. Have you ever had the unfortunate experience of observing someone else taking credit for what you have done? How did that make you

feel? What might be behind the temptation to take credit—or receive praise—for something to which we have not contributed?

2. As you look around the world today, and consider the global powers that rule, how do you feel? Hopeful? Frightened? Anxious? In what ways do you seek to remind yourself of God's ultimate control and reign over the world? How do you seek to set your sights on God's eternal kingdom in the midst of your everyday life?

OBSERVING THE TEXT

3. Notice how much of this chapter is devoted to Daniel's description and interpretation of King Nebuchadnezzar's dream. Why might the narrator have recorded such a lengthy speech from Daniel? What could this communicate to us as readers?

A God-Honoring Model, pg. 33
There is a model here for all of us in our relationships with those who do not know our God. In contrast to the self-promoting way of the world, we should constantly seek occasions to exalt and declare publicly the praises of our God. Whatever gifts and abilities we have, whatever successes we may meet with in life, all of them are ultimately the work of the one who gave us those gifts and opportunities.

4. What is the main point of the king's dream, according to Daniel? What might be some distracting debates and controversies, which could bog us down, with regard to the interpretation of the specific parts of the dream?

5. As the chapter closes, how does this part of the narrative conclude? What does the narrator seem to want the reader to notice, and what lessons might he be teaching about God?

UNDERSTANDING THE TEXT

6. How does Daniel demonstrate humility before King Nebuchadnezzar (2:26–30)? How does he use his words to point to the glory and power of God, rather than to his own wisdom and strength? How does Daniel's attitude serve as a kind of foil to that of Arioch (2:25)?

7. What is surprising about what happens in Daniel 2:31–35? How might King Nebuchadnezzar and his advisors have reacted when they heard Daniel's words? What is God demonstrating to the highest-ranking officials of Babylon as he works through Daniel?

8. What can the content and the interpretation of the king's dream (2:31–45) teach us about earthly kingdoms and political powers? What do all of these different kingdoms seem to have in common?

9. What does the final piece of the dream—the coming of the kingdom, set up by "the God of heaven" (v. 37)—teach us about the kingdom of God, as fully revealed in Jesus Christ? How ought this to give us great hope in our God?

10. What does King Nebuchadnezzar's response demonstrate about his attitude toward the God of Israel? How does his exaltation of Daniel and his friends (2:48–49) demonstrate God's faithfulness, sovereignty, and care for his people in the midst of exile?

Feet of Clay, pg. 38

The one thing that remains constant about these various kingdoms is their lust for power and their desire to dominate the world. . . . The desire to rule and crush remains undiminished throughout the sequence, but ultimately that ambition will go frustrated. In the final analysis, the kingdoms of this world, however glorious or powerful they may seem, have "feet of clay," as we say, and will not stand.

11. In what ways does this passage—both the exaltation of Daniel, because of his interpretation of the dream, and the dream itself—point us forward to the coming of Jesus Christ? What does this passage teach us about the glorious, eternal reign of Jesus?

BIBLE CONNECTIONS

12. There is perhaps no more obvious cross-reference to this passage in all of Scripture than Psalm 2, which tells of the powerful and eternal reign of the Son of God over all the nations of the world. Read that psalm and reflect on its connection to the truths revealed in Nebuchadnezzar's dream. What truths about God's kingdom do you see in both passages of Scripture?

13. In Luke 20:9–18, Jesus tells a parable to the religious leaders that clearly points to his role as the mighty "stone," or Rock, of Daniel 2. Read this parable carefully, paying close attention to verses 17–18. How does Jesus link himself to Old Testament prophecy? What are the different responses to Jesus, the Rock, that are described?

THEOLOGY CONNECTIONS

14. The dream of Daniel 2 ought to remind us that the final return and victory of Jesus is coming. Yet the timing of his return is unknown to us. The Westminster Confession of Faith explains that this is in order "that [Christians] may shake off all carnal security, and be always watchful, because they know not at what hour the Lord will come; and may be ever prepared to say, Come Lord Jesus, come quickly, Amen" (33.3). How does your study of Daniel 2 remind you to be watchful for the coming of Jesus?

15. St. Augustine, the bishop of Hippo, ministered and wrote during the decline of the Roman Empire. How might this passage from Daniel 2 have guided his understanding of the political events surrounding him? In what ways might this chapter have strengthened his faith in Christ, even in the midst of political turmoil, war, and loss of human life?

APPLYING THE TEXT

16. As you consider the opportunity that Daniel had to seek credit for himself, and yet his humble deflection of glory to God, how does this challenge you and call you to deeper humility? In what ways are you

tempted to seek glory and credit from others? How can you discipline yourself to give glory and praise to God when he graciously uses you?

17. How should the content and meaning of King Nebuchadnezzar's dream shape your perspective on global powers, world leaders, and current events? In what ways should this passage combat worry, anxiety, and restlessness about the future?

18. In what ways can you seek to have your hope shaped more and more by the coming of the eternal kingdom of Jesus Christ? How might this passage be calling you into deeper and more heartfelt worship of Jesus?

The Coming of the Rock, pg. 42

For Daniel, the coming of the Rock was a future event, something to which he could look forward in the midst of the messiness of life. For us, however, the coming of the Rock is both past and future. Jesus Christ has come into the world and established his kingdom. God calls us even now to submit to the Rock and seek first his kingdom.

PRAYER PROMPT

As you conclude your study of a passage from Daniel that we can and must apply at multiple levels, begin by praying for a heart of humility like Daniel's. Ask that God would grant you grace to willingly and joyfully deflect credit and glory from yourself to Jesus. Then pray that God would use the truths revealed in Nebuchadnezzar's dream to remind you of the glorious coming kingdom of Jesus. Ask that he would use the hope of the crucified and risen Savior's return to govern your perspective on everyday life, as you live for Jesus in word, thought, and deed.

LESSON 4

THROUGH THE FIRE

Daniel 3:1–30

THE BIG PICTURE

The difficulty of studying familiar Bible stories is that we sometimes feel like we know them already—that we've been there and done that. The story of Shadrach, Meshach, and Abednego and their refusal to bow down to Nebuchadnezzar's golden image is one such story. Yet this is more than a moralistic tale of brave young men who refuse to give in to the demands of a pagan king. In Daniel 3, we find King Nebuchadnezzar constructing a statue that is more than a statue. With intentional echoes of Genesis 11, the narrator is demonstrating the way in which the king's image has the religious unification of the Babylonian empire as its goal. Nebuchadnezzar seeks to unite his entire kingdom under the worship of this political symbol, perhaps even in a way that anticipates a reversal of the curse that followed the attempted construction of the Tower of Babel. In the face of tremendous pressure, Shadrach, Meshach, and Abednego stand alone—in both their devotion to the worship of God alone and their defiance of the king's edict. Yet even as they are thrown into the fiery furnace, they experience the salvation of God, who delivers them through the mysterious presence of a fourth figure who joins them. Amazed, King Nebuchadnezzar changes course completely and commands the nation to worship the God of these Israelite young men!

Read Daniel 3:1–30.

GETTING STARTED

1. In what ways does your culture encourage people to conform to certain viewpoints, practices, or even beliefs? What subtle or not-so-subtle "punishments" are exacted on those who do not conform?

2. Have you ever witnessed someone taking a bold stand for what is right, even in the face of tremendous opposition? If so, what was inspiring to you about it? How did you learn from such courage and conviction?

The World United, pg. 49

This act of worship was designed to reverse the consequences of the original Tower of Babel by unifying the whole world in an act of submission to this statue. When the music of a cacophony of different instruments sounded, everyone was to bow down to the statue. . . . For a moment, the whole world was united in bowing to Nebuchadnezzar's statue. The curse of Babel had, it seemed, successfully been reversed.

OBSERVING THE TEXT

3. How does the golden image, which Nebuchadnezzar constructs, remind us of the previous passage we studied (see Daniel 2:31–35)? What might the narrator be communicating by placing these chapters in succession?

4. What might Nebuchadnezzar be attempting to achieve by commanding everyone to worship the image he has built? What clues do you get in the passage as to the motives of the Babylonian king?

5. What do you notice about the words of Shadrach, Meshach, and Abednego in Daniel 3? How are they firm and strong in their commitment? How do they demonstrate humility and respect toward the king? How do they bear witness to a deep trust in God?

Standing Alone, pg. 50

It is worth noticing that there were only three men in the whole crowd who refused to bow down to Nebuchadnezzar's statue. This highlights the fact that standing up for God will often be a lonely activity. There are times in every life when to do what is right we cannot simply hide in the crowd; we have to stand more or less alone.

UNDERSTANDING THE TEXT

6. How does the narrator describe the "image of gold" that Nebuchadnez-zar constructs? What is surprising about the penalty for not bowing in worship to the image, and what does that tell you about the political significance of this statue (3:6)?

7. In the report that is brought to King Nebuchadnezzar concerning the young men from Israel who refuse to bow down (3:8–12), what motives are attached to their behavior? How are they accused before the king?

8. What does the text make clear about King Nebuchadnezzar's response to the three Israelite men and their refusal to bow down (3:13–14)? How does he challenge them, threaten them, and forcefully ask them to reconsider their position?

9. What is shocking about the young men's response to the king (3:16–18)? What seems to be uncertain in their minds, according to their words? What convictions guide their behavior and their resistance?

10. The surprising climax of the passage comes in 3:24–25, as Nebuchadnezzar leaps to his feet in amazement. What causes the king to call out in surprise? How ought we to understand the presence of the fourth "man" in the furnace with Shadrach, Meshach, and Abednego (3:25)? How does this point us to the coming of Jesus Christ, who is called "God with us" (Matt. 1:23)?

11. In Daniel 3:26–27, how does the narrator call additional attention to the miraculous work of God in these events? How does this passage lead to the worship of God as the absolutely unique and sovereign God above all gods? What effect does the salvation of these three men have on King Nebuchadnezzar?

God's Personal Emissary, pg. 56

[The fourth man] is a physical demonstration of God's presence with believers in their distress. God did not simply rescue his servants from the fire, he sent his personal emissary to pass through the fire with them, a presence that takes richer dimensions in the New Testament, when God comes to dwell physically with us as Immanuel.

BIBLE CONNECTIONS

12. Many biblical scholars point out that Nebuchadnezzar's golden image was likely constructed near the spot where the Tower of Babel (Gen. 11) was built. Take a moment to reacquaint yourself with that account by reading Genesis 11:1–9. What similarities do you observe between the mind-set of the people in Genesis 11 and the probable motivation of the king of Babylon? What do you notice about God's response in both narratives?

13. Read Acts 4:13–22, which could be considered as an additional biblical example of "civil disobedience." What direct command do Peter and John disobey? Why do they disobey it? How would you compare the motivations of the three young men in Daniel 3 with those of Peter and John in Acts 4?

THEOLOGY CONNECTIONS

14. In the wake of tremendous pressure from the leaders of the Roman Catholic Church in his day, the great Reformer Martin Luther insisted on a biblical view of justification by faith alone. Explaining to a great crowd gathered at the Diet of Worms that his "conscience is captive to the Word of God," Luther refused to recant or turn from his teaching.[1]

1. See Roland H. Bainton, *The Reformation of the Sixteenth Century* (Boston: Beacon, 1965), 61, quoted in the REC commentary, 50.

How was Luther following in the footsteps of the three young men in Daniel 3? What was the ultimate result of Luther's boldness and courage?

15. The Heidelberg Catechism explains that the second commandment teaches us: "That we in no way make any image of God nor worship him in any other way than has been commanded in God's Word" (Q&A 96). How are we tempted to worship God in ways that are *not* commanded in his Word? Why is right worship of God—and of him alone—of such fundamental importance?

APPLYING THE TEXT

16. While most of us will probably not face a life-or-death demand to worship a statue, we are pulled in much more subtle ways toward conformity, acceptance of cultural standards, or even certain forms of worship. What do these pressures look like in your life? How are you pressured to give honor or "worship" to things other than your Lord?

17. How should the presence of the fourth man in the furnace with Shadrach, Meshach, and Abednego encourage you about the character of God? What is God teaching you about his compassionate heart for his people as they endure hardship?

18. In what ways can you avoid a simply moralistic application of this passage? How does Daniel 3 call you to imitate these brave and faithful young men, but also to trust the finished work of the Savior who endured the ultimate suffering in your place?

PRAYER PROMPT

As you close this time of study in Daniel 3, ask God to embolden you to stand courageously for him in the midst of cultural and societal pressures to conform. Pray that God would indeed give you courage, fearlessness, and an undivided heart of worship toward him! But pray also that our gracious God would remind you of his presence with you in the midst of the trials of life. The Son of God came near; he dwelt among his people; he endured the fiery wrath of God in our stead! Thank your Father for his salvation through Christ; ask him to enable you to boldly stand for him in every trial.

LESSON 5

THE FALL AND RISE OF KING NEBUCHADNEZZAR

Daniel 4:1–37

THE BIG PICTURE

Daniel 4 begins and ends with exclamations of unexpected praise to the God of Israel—coming from the lips of the pagan King Nebuchadnezzar of Babylon! It is a chapter that forces us to reckon with the power of God, who is no tribal deity, but rules over the mightiest of kings and the greatest of earthly kingdoms. As before in the narrative, King Nebuchadnezzar is troubled by a dream. This time he calls immediately for Daniel to give him its interpretation. The tree in the king's dream, which represents his glorious rule over Babylon, is stripped bare, with its fruit scattered. Daniel explains the dream's meaning: King Nebuchadnezzar will be humiliated and humbled before God because of his pride, until he recognizes that the Most High rules the world and deserves glory and praise. The events foretold in the dream soon take place: King Nebuchadnezzar, following a moment of self-indulgent arrogance, is driven into a humiliating madness, until he lifts up his voice to praise and acknowledge God at the chapter's close. The king's "majesty and splendor" are returned to him (4:36), even as he commits himself to the ongoing praise and honor of "the King of heaven" (4:37).

Read Daniel 4:1–37.

GETTING STARTED

1. Why might you affirm that pride is one of the most dangerous and deadly sins? In what ways have you observed that arrogance and pride can wreak havoc in one's life, relationships, or profession? How have you battled prideful tendencies in your own heart and mind?

2. In what ways can excessive pride lead to one's downfall? How can a fall, though, sometimes lead to greater humility, joy, and growth? Can you describe a time when you grew in your faith through the experience of failure or a deeply humbling situation?

A Dramatic Transformation, pg. 64

In Nebuchadnezzar's case, the transformation required the stripping away of everything in which he once gloried. He began the chapter with everything he desired, contented and prosperous, at home in his palace. . . . Nebuchadnezzar was, quite literally, the lord of all that he surveyed.

OBSERVING THE TEXT

3. As you read through the first three verses of Daniel 4, why might you be tempted to think that these verses belong with the previous chapter? How might these verses be functioning, assuming that they do indeed belong with the narrative of chapter 4?

4. What is surprising about the opening words of King Nebuchadnezzar (4:1–3)? Why is this such a shocking transformation, especially considering his early behavior and commands? How do the closing verses of the chapter echo these opening verses?

5. How does the dream of the king in this passage repeat some of the themes of his dream in chapter 2? What are the divine truths that God is continually communicating to Daniel, King Nebuchadnezzar, and the kingdom of Babylon through these dreams?

UNDERSTANDING THE TEXT

6. As King Nebuchadnezzar is again troubled by a dream, he turns to Daniel (Belteshazzar) for help and interpretation. What do his words indicate about his estimation of Daniel's wisdom and character (4:8–9,

18)? How does this demonstrate to us the ongoing work of God in Daniel's life?

7. What are the contents of the king's dream, which he describes in 4:10–17? Why might this dream have been so troubling to him, particularly given the meaning of the dream that Daniel had previously interpreted for him?

8. How does 4:15 provide hope for the tree—even beyond the humiliating stripping and cutting? How does this foreshadow the conclusion of the chapter and the actual events of Nebuchadnezzar's life?

9. According to Daniel, what is the specific purpose of the humiliation of this tree in the dream (4:24–25)? What does this explicit purpose imply about the mind-set and attitude of King Nebuchadnezzar? Why might his attitude have been such an affront to God?

10. What heart attitude is revealed through the pompous words of Nebuchadnezzar as he gazes out over his kingdom (4:28–30)? What do his

words imply about his response to the message of his dream and the accompanying warning from Daniel?

11. How is the judgment on King Nebuchadnezzar described in the text (4:33)? What leads to his ultimate restoration? How would you describe his response to God as the chapter closes? In what ways does this give us a model for Christian repentance and humble faith in Jesus Christ?

BIBLE CONNECTIONS

12. Interestingly, what happens to King Nebuchadnezzar in Daniel 4 is simultaneously happening at a national level to the people of Israel; they too are being stripped, pruned, and humiliated through the discipline of exile in Babylon. Take a moment to read Isaiah 6:11–13. What similarities do you find between God's words to his people and the contents of the dream in Daniel 4?

The Essence of Humility, pg. 71
It is significant that the end of Nebuchadnezzar's humbling and the return of his reason came when he took his eyes off himself and lifted them to heaven in an act of supplication and dependence. This looking away from oneself is the essence of true humility, and the means by which we can distinguish it from the counterfeit form.

13. Jesus Christ, speaking to a proud and self-sufficient church in first-century Laodicea, rebukes and invites them with these words: "For you say, I am rich, I have prospered, and I need nothing, not realizing that you are wretched, pitiable, poor, blind, and naked. I counsel you to buy from me gold refined by fire, so that you may be rich, and white garments so that you may clothe yourself and the shame of your nakedness may not be seen, and salve to anoint your eyes, so that you may see" (Rev. 3:17–18). How does Jesus call for a response similar to that of King Nebuchadnezzar in this passage?

THEOLOGY CONNECTIONS

14. The Westminster Confession of Faith describes true repentance as involving the sinner's apprehension of "the filthiness and odiousness of his sins, as contrary to the holy nature, and righteous law of God; and upon the apprehension of his mercy in Christ to such as are penitent, so grieves for, and hates his sins, as to turn from them all unto God" (15.20). How is this reality vividly portrayed in both the madness and the repentance of King Nebuchadnezzar?

15. As the Reformer John Calvin once wrote, "The human mind is, so to speak, a perpetual forge of idols" (*Institutes*, 1.11.8). Why is this such an important realization as we search our own hearts for signs of pride, arrogance, and self-sufficiency—or even self-worship?

APPLYING THE TEXT

16. While very few of us (probably!) can, like Nebuchadnezzar, gaze out over massive kingdoms ruled by us, we can still turn quickly to attitudes of pride, arrogance, and self-sufficiency. What does this generally look like for you? How can you pursue true humility as a follower of Jesus Christ and battle the prideful tendencies of your heart?

17. In what ways is King Nebuchadnezzar's repentance at the end of this chapter a model for the way you approach the throne of grace as a sinner? How can his beastly and filthy humiliation expand our picture of our desperate need for the grace of Jesus Christ?

18. Why is King Nebuchadnezzar's ultimate restoration an encouraging reminder of God's grace and mercy? In what ways do you need to be reminded of the need for humility, but also of the hope of future glory—and even our ultimate reign with Christ as his people?

The Humbling Gospel, pg. 72

The gospel is an intrinsically humbling message. The only way for us to enter God's kingdom is with empty hands, lifting our eyes to heaven and confessing our desperate need of a savior. By nature, that is hard for all of us.

PRAYER PROMPT

Daniel 4 shows us the power of God to humble even the most powerful king of the known world. He is indeed "the King of heaven"—before whom, one day, every knee shall bow. Today, pray that God would chase prideful arrogance from your heart and grant you humility and joyful worship toward him. Ask him to give you the ongoing gift of repentance, as you trust the gracious work of Jesus Christ, your Savior. Pray that he would give you hope in his ultimate and final exaltation of all his redeemed people!

LESSON 6

WEIGHED AND FOUND WANTING

Daniel 5:1–31

THE BIG PICTURE

Chapter 5 of the book of Daniel takes us out of the reign of Nebuchadnezzar and into the reign of his son Belshazzar. While the text does not give many explicit details about the reign of this young king, the careful reader may assume that he is more partyer than warrior! Our introduction to Belshazzar comes in the midst of a raucous party, complete with excessive drinking, pompous decorations, and the worship of idols (5:1–4). In the midst of the merrymaking, however, we read of a frightening occurrence: a human hand begins writing on the wall of the room (5:5). Terrified, the young king—prompted by the queen mother—does what his father had done so many times before: he calls for Daniel. Daniel interprets the mysterious words on the wall, which declare the downfall of King Belshazzar, who has been "weighed" by God and found "wanting" (5:27). As Daniel is rewarded by the king for his wisdom, Belshazzar enjoys a few more hours of life before he is killed and his kingdom is overthrown by Darius the Mede. This startling passage points back to Nebuchadnezzar's dream of the statue, even as it reminds the reader of God's sovereignty over the rise and fall of kings and nations. In the midst of this rise and fall, faithful Daniel is kept safe by God and used by him in mighty ways!

Read Daniel 5:1–31.

GETTING STARTED

1. By what standards are nations and rulers of nations generally judged by our world today? What are typical markers of success? How do you judge political rulers and leaders as you look back on them in history?

2. What occurrences in our world today tend to make you long for God's judgment—or even for the return of Christ? In what ways do you struggle to understand God's timing, as well as the seeming delay of his justice?

The Sole Event Worth Mentioning, pg. 79

Greek historians like Herodotus recorded many such lavish feasts on the part of the Babylonians, and this was one of the best. Everyone was dressed in his finest clothes and the tables were set with the most ornate silverware. Yet by focusing our attention on this elaborate feast as the sole event worth mentioning in his account, the narrator subtly underlines for us the emptiness of the remainder of Belshazzar's life.

OBSERVING THE TEXT

3. What do you learn—simply from careful observation of the text—about the character of King Belshazzar? What seems to be most important to him? What does he value, based on his words and actions?

4. What can you deduce about Daniel's role in the political life of Babylon in the days leading up to the events of chapter 5? What is significant about Daniel's absence from the reign of Belshazzar up to this point?

5. How do Daniel's words (and tone) to Belshazzar differ from his words (and tone) to King Nebuchadnezzar? What do you notice that is different about these two kings?

UNDERSTANDING THE TEXT

6. How does the narrator set up this account in the first four verses of the passage? To what does he draw the reader's attention, and what can we learn from this?

7. What effect does the appearance of the "human hand" have on King Belshazzar (5:5–6)? What is his immediate response? How does the queen mother offer help, and how does she describe the character and capability of Daniel? What do her words seem to imply to the king about his ignorance of Daniel?

8. Before Daniel interprets the handwriting on the wall, he makes a somewhat lengthy speech to King Belshazzar (5:17–23). What point is he making to the king? How is he contrasting the king's attitude toward God with that of his father?

9. How does Daniel explain the meaning of the words written on the wall (5:25–28)? In what ways does the interpretation relate to the interpretation of Nebuchadnezzar's dream of the giant statue (Daniel 2)? How ought we to view Belshazzar's party, in light of the meaning of his dream?

Divine Foreshadowing, pg. 83

The sequence of decay that the vision of Daniel 2 anticipated for world history—moving from gold to silver to bronze to fragile feet of iron and clay—found a foreshadowing within the history of the Babylonian empire. Like the sequence of weights in the oracle, the once mighty kingdom became insubstantial and was ultimately blown away by the judgment of God.

10. What lessons do we learn about God from this passage? How and why is God bringing judgment on Belshazzar and his kingdom?

11. Daniel 5:30–31 gives a brief summary of the overthrow of Babylon, the execution of Belshazzar, and the transfer of power to Darius the Mede. How does the brevity of this summary highlight the main point of the passage? What questions do we have, as readers, about the future of Daniel and God's plan for him?

BIBLE CONNECTIONS

12. In Psalm 1, the righteous are contrasted with the wicked; the righteous have lasting, tree-like strength, but the wicked are ultimately transient and insignificant. Look back at Psalm 1 and consider the picture of the wicked as "chaff" that the wind blows away. How is this reality demonstrated in the events of Daniel 5?

13. Daniel 5 points us to the reality of God's sovereignty in salvation, even as Daniel's speech describes the different responses to God from Belshazzar and Nebuchadnezzar. Read Romans 9:15–18; what does

Paul remind his readers of God's sovereign choice in salvation? Why can this be a difficult reality for us to accept?

THEOLOGY CONNECTIONS

14. Chapter 5 of the Westminster Confession of Faith begins with these words: "God the great Creator of all things doth uphold, direct, dispose, and govern all creatures, actions, and things, from the greatest even to the least, by his most wise and holy providence" (5.1). In what ways does Daniel 5 demonstrate the mysterious and powerful providence of God? How does God actively "direct" and "dispose" creatures and actions in this passage?

15. Augustine of Hippo observes, "The earthly city glories in itself, the Heavenly City glories in the Lord" (*City of God*, 14.28). How does Daniel 5 present a disgusting picture of an earthly city glorying in itself? What does God's swift judgment on Belshazzar's sumptuous banquet remind us of the transience of the earthly city—and, by contrast, the eternality of the Heavenly City?

APPLYING THE TEXT

16. What does this chapter of Daniel tell us about how we should consider human power and wealth? How should this passage serve as a great warning to us?

17. In what ways does this passage cause you to adjust your perspective concerning the transience of human empires and national powers? How might you adjust your prayers to God in light of this passage?

18. How can this passage drive you to a deeper trust and hope in the mercy of God, through Jesus Christ his Son? How does Daniel 5 remind you that Jesus is your only hope?

The Mercy of God, pg. 87
We should therefore be astonished that God continues to show us mercy. Taken together, Daniel 4 and 5 show us God's utter sovereignty in salvation. He showed mercy to King Nebuchadnezzar in spite of his earlier persecution of God's people. He humbled him and brought him to the point where he truly understood the reality of God's power over him and bowed the knee before him. Yet there was no such mercy for Belshazzar.

PRAYER PROMPT

As you bring your study of this passage to a close and approach God in prayer, begin by asking him to give you the gift of his perspective on earthly power, wealth, and pomp. Ask him to show you more and more the transience of worldly glory, in contrast to the eternal glory of knowing Christ Jesus the King. Pray that he would guard you from obsession with power and prominence and grant you humility as you trust his ways, his justice, and his timing.

LESSON 7

IN THE ANGEL'S DEN

Daniel 6:1–28

THE BIG PICTURE

As Daniel 6 opens, with King Darius now on the throne, we discover that Daniel has had a kind of resurgence in leadership after being largely neglected and ignored by King Belshazzar. As part of his rule over his kingdom, Darius appoints 120 "satraps," with three top officials overseeing the entire group; Daniel is one of these three (6:2). In this we find the theme of God's faithfulness to Daniel—and to his Word—continuing in the days of exile. Even so, Daniel clearly is not without his enemies. Many of the other officials view him with envy; they devise a plot to bring about his ruin (which they know will have to be tied to his faith in God). The satraps and officials play upon the ego of King Darius, enticing him into decreeing that no one in the kingdom should pray to anyone but him for thirty days. Daniel, true to his normal practices, prays openly and publicly to God, and is dragged before the king, who tries unsuccessfully to find a way to reverse his decree. Ultimately, Daniel receives the punishment: he is cast into a den of lions, where God miraculously delivers him through the hand of his "angel" (6:22). King Darius responds by again exalting Daniel and throwing his adversaries into the den of the lions, where they are quickly devoured. The chapter concludes with a stunning decree from the pagan king, acknowledging the ultimate reign of the "God of Daniel," who alone is "the living God" (6:26–27).

Read Daniel 6:1–28.

GETTING STARTED

1. What is difficult about navigating life in the systems and cultures of the world, while remaining faithfully committed to Jesus Christ and God's Word? Where have you sensed dissonance between God's values and the value of your culture? How have you seen this in your profession, your neighborhood, or your social sphere?

2. While most of us have not faced the threat of death for publicly worshiping Jesus, what other threats or dangers might we face when we speak God's Word publicly, acknowledge the gospel boldly, or insist that Jesus is the only way to salvation?

Daniel's Enemies, pg. 93

Daniel's goodness did not win him friends on all sides. Instead, his faithfulness to his duty to God and man made him powerful enemies. Some sought to bring him down, probably both because they were jealous of his success and because his incorruptibility was restricting their ability to use the system for their own personal benefit. Isn't that always the way it is?

OBSERVING THE TEXT

3. What do you notice about Daniel's reputation with the people around him, as this chapter opens? What do they acknowledge about him? How does that impact their strategy for attacking him?

4. How would you characterize King Darius's estimation of Daniel throughout this chapter? What seems to be taught here about the attractiveness of godly character and wisdom?

5. In what ways is the conclusion of this account meant to surprise us as readers? What is shocking about Daniel's deliverance? What is even more shocking about the king's response to Daniel's deliverance, as well as his declaration to the kingdom?

UNDERSTANDING THE TEXT

6. How is Daniel's ascension described in the opening verses of this chapter? How does Darius's response to Daniel differ from that of Belshazzar

(see Daniel 5)? What are we learning about God's faithfulness to Daniel and his hand in Daniel's life?

7. What seems to be motivating the high officials and the satraps who hate Daniel and seek his downfall (6:4–5)? How can this help us to understand opposition to the Christian faith, as well as hatred of Christians themselves?

8. Why is the decree, suggested to Darius by the satraps, appealing to the king (6:6–9)? How might Daniel have sought to escape the consequences for disobeying the edict? Instead, what does Daniel do, and what can we learn from his actions (6:10–11)? What might God be seeking to do through Daniel's conviction and arrest?

Saved through Trials, pg. 97

[God's] purpose was not to save Daniel *from* trials but to save Daniel *through* trials. Just as was earlier the case with Shadrach, Meshach, and Abednego, there were lessons that Daniel and those around him would learn, that could be learned only by Daniel going into the den of lions.

9. What is surprising about the king's words to Daniel in 6:16? How does God answer this "prayer" of King Darius in the following verses? In what way is Darius's night (6:18) contrasted with the peaceful demeanor of Daniel in this passage?

10. To whom does Daniel attribute his rescue from the lions? What do we learn about God's preservation of his people from this account? How does 6:23 emphasize God's overwhelming and comprehensive care for Daniel?

11. How is God bringing glory to himself through these events (6:26–27)? What are we learning about God's heart for his people, as well as for the nations of the world? How does this point us to the gospel, particularly as we consider Daniel's innocence, death, and deliverance, and the resulting praise given to God?

BIBLE CONNECTIONS

12. While Daniel 6 records real events that happened in the life of Daniel, long before the time of Christ, we must acknowledge the way in which this account prefigures the betrayal, trial, death, burial, and miraculous resurrection of our Savior. Using your knowledge of the gospel accounts of Jesus' trial, death, and resurrection, describe some of the similarities between them and this account in Daniel 6. How is Daniel a type of Christ?

13. Read Hebrews 11:32–38, which makes reference to this passage in Daniel, along with many other instances of faith at work in the lives of God's people. What unites Daniel with the faithful people of God in every age, despite different stories and circumstances?

Parallels to Christ, pgs. 103–4

Like Daniel, Jesus was falsely accused by his enemies and brought before a ruler, Pontius Pilate, who sought unsuccessfully to deliver him from his fate, before handing him over to a violent death. Like Daniel, Jesus was condemned to die, and his body was placed into a sealed pit so that his situation could not be changed by human intervention. . . . God raised him from the dead, precisely because the heavenly tribunal found him not guilty.

THEOLOGY CONNECTIONS

14. One additional theme that emerges from Daniel 6 is that of civil disobedience; Daniel disobeys the edict of King Darius when it clashes with faithful obedience to God's Word. John Calvin writes of Daniel's decision: "For earthly princes lay aside their power when they rise up against God" (*Commentaries on Daniel*, 1:382). How are Calvin's words helpful in establishing a basic principle of civil disobedience, which Daniel applies in this chapter?

15. The Heidelberg Catechism reminds us of the importance of prayer with these words: "Prayer is the most important part of the thankfulness which God requires of us" (Q&A 116). How might this conviction have guided Daniel's devotion to prayer in Daniel 6?

APPLYING THE TEXT

16. How can we learn from Daniel's "dual citizenship"—the fact that he prospers in Babylonian political leadership, while remaining doggedly devoted to praying to God and worshiping him? In what ways might we apply this to our work in our culture today?

17. What is challenging to you, personally, about this passage? How should Daniel's bold commitment to prayer and worship—even under threat of death—guide our courageous commitment to Christ in the midst of opposition?

18. How can you, as a follower of Jesus, more faithfully live for God as an "exile" in this world? In what ways should this passage shape your attitude toward persecution, hardship, and struggle as you live for Christ? How do you need to be reminded of God's heart for the nations?

PRAYER PROMPT

Daniel 6 shows us Daniel flourishing in the midst of exile, as he clings to bold faith in God even when threatened with death. Today, as you close your study, ask God for boldness and courage to cling to Christ in all trials. Even more than that, pray that he would deepen your trust in your Savior, who, though innocent, suffered death in your place and was raised gloriously to life for your justification!

LESSON 8

THE TRIUMPH OF THE SON OF MAN

Daniel 7:1-28

THE BIG PICTURE

As we come to our study of Daniel 7, it will be good to acknowledge that we have entered a different part of the book—along with a different literary genre. The first six chapters of Daniel fall within the genre of Old Testament narrative; the second six chapters are generally classified as *apocalyptic* literature, which refers to a "revealing" of God's cosmic purposes for both final judgment and the ultimate salvation of his people. This apocalyptic section of the book of Daniel begins with a dream in chapter 7, through which Daniel is confronted with a series of visions (7:1). We find that this dream takes place during the reign of King Belshazzar, so we have obviously moved back in time from chapter 6. In the dream, Daniel first receives visions of four terrible beasts rising up from the sea. The beasts are judged and defeated by "the Ancient of Days," after which a figure called the "son of man" is exalted—given dominion and rule over all the earth (7:13–14). While still in his dream, Daniel asks for the interpretation, and he receives the explanation: the four beasts represent mighty kings who will rise up to reign, destroy, and dominate. But the dream tells of the ultimate defeat of these evil powers by a good God, who reigns through his Son and will ultimately deliver his eternal and glorious kingdom to "the saints of the Most High" (7:27).

Read Daniel 7:1-28.

GETTING STARTED

1. What recent movies, books, or television shows have dealt with end-of-the-world scenarios? Why is there such a cultural fascination with epic and apocalyptic story lines and plots?

2. In your past study of biblical apocalyptic literature, what has been most challenging for you? What struggles, questions, or frustrations have you experienced as you studied the book of Revelation, for example? Why is this type of biblical literature so difficult for us?

A Theology of Hope, pg. 107

Apocalyptic literature thus proclaims a theology of hope to those whom the world has marginalized: it reminds us that God is presently on the throne and that he will ultimately triumph. In the meantime, whatever the present cost may be in terms of suffering, obedience to God is the only way.

OBSERVING THE TEXT

3. How have dreams played a key part in the book of Daniel thus far? How has God used dreams? How is Daniel's dream similar to the dreams of the kings in this book? How is it different?

4. Who are the main characters in Daniel's vision? How do they interact with one another? How would you summarize the basic "plot" of his dream?

5. Based on your initial reading of this chapter, what seems to be the big picture, or main point, of the vision that Daniel receives? What does God seem to intend for him to understand?

UNDERSTANDING THE TEXT

6. What do you notice about the description of the "beasts" whom Daniel sees (7:1–7)? What is the significance of the fact that they rise up out

of the sea? What is different about the fourth beast? How would you react to this part of the dream if you were Daniel?

7. While the exact identity of the beasts (representing "kings") is not given to Daniel, or to us, the vision certainly makes it clear what their ultimate destiny will be. What is their end? What is God's role in their downfall, and what does this show us about God?

8. Why might the vision from God have given Daniel such a detailed view of the heavenly "court" of judgment, as well as of God himself (7:9–12)? What do we learn about the reality of God's holiness and judgment in these verses? How should these verses challenge and convict us?

God, Not Monsters, pg. 112

It is essential for us to notice that the focus of the chapter as a whole is not on the monsters themselves. After all, the purpose of the passage is not to give us nightmares but to calm our nightmares. The focus of Daniel 7 is rather on the coming day of divine judgment, when these monsters will finally receive justice and God will win the final victory.

9. How is the coming of the "son of man" described in this passage (7:13–14)? What do you note about his description, as well as the people's response to him? How does this vision point forward to Jesus Christ, who is both human and divine?

10. What is God's purpose for his "saints" in the midst of his judgment on his enemies (7:22, 27)? How does this demonstrate God's love and mercy in the midst of his justice and punishment?

11. How does the vision of Daniel (and the chapter) conclude? What seems to be the final application for Daniel? What truths are confirmed for God's people at the close of the chapter?

BIBLE CONNECTIONS

12. While there is danger in delving into endless debate about the identity of the "beasts" mentioned in Daniel 7, the reality of powerful enemies arraying themselves against God is well attested throughout Scripture. Read Revelation 13:1–4 and compare it to Daniel's dream. What is similar about the beast? From where does it rise?

13. As you may know, "Son of Man" is a favorite phrase by which Jesus refers to himself in the Gospels. Based on Daniel 7, what is Jesus communicating about his divinity when he uses that title? How does this title also point to his true humanity?

THEOLOGY CONNECTIONS

14. The Westminster Confession of Faith speaks to the dual role of the final day of judgment, as it shows both God's grace and his justice: "The end of God's appointing this day is for the manifestation of the glory of his mercy, in the eternal salvation of the elect; and of his justice, in the damnation of the reprobate, who are wicked and disobedient" (33.2). How are both God's mercy and his justice evident in Daniel 7?

15. Many earnest and thoughtful Christians disagree about some of the precise details and timing of the return of Jesus and the final judgment. Even Martin Luther, the great Reformer, once hopefully suggested that Christ would return within one hundred years (*Table Talk*, trans. Hazlitt, 325). What precise details about the final judgment are withheld from us in Daniel 7? What big-picture truths are clearly taught?

APPLYING THE TEXT

16. Despite the somewhat frightening aspects of Daniel's dream, why ought this chapter to be a deeply encouraging one for the people of God? How should you be encouraged and strengthened in your faith as you read and study Daniel 7?

17. How should this apocalyptic vision shape your perspective of world powers—and particularly evil powers? How should it shape your view of the ultimate justice of God?

18. How should Daniel 7 strengthen your hope in Jesus Christ and revitalize your worship of him? In what ways does Daniel's vision enhance your vision of your Savior?

Let the World Do Its Worst, pg. 120

If God is my judge and the Son of Man is my savior, then let the world do its worst. Ultimately, the world has no power to hurt me, and I know that after the world has done its worst, God will welcome me into his very best. The Lord has a gracious inheritance stored up for me, along with all of the saints, a kingdom that is mine by grace alone, through faith in Christ alone.

PRAYER PROMPT

While Daniel 7 presents us with a vision that could be a frightful nightmare, the intended effect on us, as God's people, is not fear, but comfort. God will indeed judge the world, but his eternal kingdom will belong to those who have given themselves in faith to the Son of Man. As you close your study today, pray that God would strengthen your faith and hope in Jesus Christ—your Savior and your Judge. Ask him for proper perspective on the powers of this world, as well as his coming judgment. Pray that he would give you endurance, obedience, and faithfulness until the last day.

LESSON 9

WAITING IN THE VALLEY OF DARKNESS

Daniel 8:1–27

THE BIG PICTURE

Like the previous chapter, Daniel 8 again records a dreamlike vision given by God to Daniel, along with an accompanying explanation from an angelic figure. Unlike chapter 7, though, this dream comes with a slightly more specific interpretation. Daniel's dream begins with a vision of a powerful ram with two horns—one shorter than the other. These horns are later interpreted to be the kings of Media and Persia (8:20). As Daniel watches, the two-horned ram is charged by a much more powerful one-horned goat, which crushes and defeats the ram, leaving it helpless. This goat, representing the empire of Greece, produces four horns, which are interpreted to be the far less powerful kingdoms that arise in the wake of the Greek empire. The final part of the vision reveals one last horn, which emerges after the four weaker horns. This represents the rise of a final, powerful king—perhaps Antiochus Epiphanes—who will desecrate the worship of the people of God and even rebel against God himself (8:25). But God will ultimately throw down this imposter, along with all similarly satanic assaults on his kingdom. He will restore his rightful rule over his people, as well as the purity of their worship of him. The dream of chapter 8 leaves Daniel more troubled than the vision of chapter 7; he lies sick for many days, waiting without full understanding. God is continuing to reveal

79

his final judgment on the rebellious world, along with the final preservation and salvation of his saints.

Read Daniel 8:1–27.

GETTING STARTED

1. Think about some of the darkest moments of your life—spiritually, emotionally, relationally, or physically. Why was it difficult to wait on God? How did you seek to pursue patience, obedience, and ongoing faith in God's promises?

2. How often do you think about the return of Christ and the end of the world? Do you tend to be *too* obsessed with end-time prognostication? Or could you perhaps be *more* regularly thoughtful about the inevitable return of Christ?

A New Focus, pg. 124

The earlier vision expressed universal and ultimate realities in the language of symbolism rather than history, and therefore appropriately took place in an undefined location, beside the great Sea. . . . In the vision of chapter 8, however, we focus on the particularities of specific and easily identifiable historical figures and kingdoms.

OBSERVING THE TEXT

3. How is this vision different from Daniel's dream in the previous chapter? What aspects of this dream are more specific (less general and universal)? What might this tell us?

4. Describe the distinct parts of this vision and the progression from one aspect to the next. What might be the significance of the animals and the horns?

5. Note the explanation of the dream given to Daniel. What is explained clearly, and what is left unexplained? What is Daniel's state of mind as the chapter closes? Why might this be?

UNDERSTANDING THE TEXT

6. What happens in the altercation between the two-horned ram and the charging, one-horned goat (8:3–8)? What kind of historical events

might be symbolically described here? What hints do we have as to the meaning from King Nebuchadnezzar's earlier dream?

7. How does the vision of the "little horn" demonstrate that the "ram" and the "goat" were merely a foretaste of something greater to come (8:8–12)? What cosmic actions are attached to this little horn? With whom might we be led to identify the horn's actions and attacks?

8. What does Daniel learn about the meaning of the vision in 8:13–19? What is explicitly explained? What remains somewhat unclear?

God's Victory Affirmed, pg. 133

Daniel 8 affirms God's victory even in the face of the coming darkness of the days of Antiochus Epiphanes. If God's purposes were not thwarted by that period of rebellion and defilement, then they will certainly never be thwarted by our personal experience of unfaithfulness or persecution.

9. How is the rebellion of a powerful human figure described with cosmic and heavenly language in 8:24–26? Why is it helpful to us to understand political victory and domination in these terms?

10. How is this powerful figure ultimately defeated (8:25)? In what ways does this future defeat of evil earthly powers relate to previous dreams in the book of Daniel?

11. What physical effect does this dream have on Daniel (8:27)? Why does he say that he "was appalled by the vision and did not understand it," even after receiving the interpretation from the angel? What might this verse have to teach us about aspects of God's plan, purposes, and ways?

BIBLE CONNECTIONS

12. For the first readers of the book of Daniel, these visions may have filled them with a sense that the end of all things was quite near. But now, more than 2,500 years later, Christ has not yet returned. Take a moment

and read 2 Peter 3:8–10. How does Peter explain the "delay" of Jesus? To what truths must Christians hold, according to Peter?

13. As Christians, we know that the cross of Jesus Christ brings us forgiveness for our sins and the hope of eternal life. It also reveals God's ultimate trials over Satan. Take a moment to read Colossians 2:15. What does God do to the "rulers and authorities" through the cross of his Son? Why ought this to give Christians great hope?

THEOLOGY CONNECTIONS

14. The Heidelberg Catechism reminds us of our ultimate comfort in Christ: "He has fully paid for all my sins with his precious blood, and has set me free from the tyranny of the devil. He also watches over me in such a way that not a hair can fall from my head without the will of my Father in heaven; in fact, all things must work together for my salvation" (Q&A 1). How do these truths point us to *ultimate* comfort in the midst of *temporal* struggles—and even terrors such as the ones mentioned in Daniel 8?

15. This is a chapter whose ending (8:27) leaves Daniel sick and confused. We can often feel that way about the endless debates that Christians sometimes have about matters of the end times and the timing of the return of Jesus Christ. What essential truths must Christians affirm

about the return of Jesus Christ and the last days? About what details do Bible-believing Christians sometimes disagree?

APPLYING THE TEXT

16. What instruction does this chapter provide as we think about the final day of judgment? On what are we supposed to focus? What does Daniel 8:26 have to say about the timing of this final day, at least for this book's original audience?

17. How are you tempted to doubt the justice of God as you look around the world today? In what ways can you remind yourself—and others—of the coming final judgment of the Prince of Peace, Jesus Christ? What might this look like in the context of your local church?

God's Answer at the Cross, pg. 134
The cross is thus the place where God gave his final answer to our rebellion and transgression, as well as to Satan's enmity. At the cross, Jesus took upon himself the full weight of all our transgression and rebellion, dealing once and for all with our sin. If ever there was a "time of wrath," it was during those six hours when Jesus hung on the cross, bearing the wrath of God against our wickedness and idolatry. His devastation there brought God's wrath against our sin to a final end.

18. In what ways should the ending of this chapter—particularly 8:27—
help you understand the importance of *waiting* in the Christian life?
With what attitude and expectation do we wait for the return of Christ?
Why might God want us to wait for his provision of relief in other areas
of our lives as well?

PRAYER PROMPT

Daniel's vision in this chapter leaves him restless—and even physically sick.
Despite being given some interpretation, we find Daniel waiting on God
for his final explanation and revelation of his plan. There is a lesson for us
in this, even as we wait for God to make all things right at the return of his
Son, Jesus Christ. Today, pray that God would give you patience, hope, and
joy as you patiently wait for him. Ask that he would give you perseverance
to endure, trusting in the final victory of your Lord and Savior.

LESSON 10

PRAYING AND HOPING
IN THE DARKNESS

Daniel 9:1–27

THE BIG PICTURE

Daniel 9 opens, not with another vision of Daniel, but essentially with Daniel doing his "devotions." He is reading the prophet Jeremiah and considering the seventy-year exile for God's people that is promised. Daniel's response is to offer an earnest and heartfelt prayer on behalf of God's people. He confesses their sins and acknowledges their overwhelming guilt before God (9:3–15). He admits that God is justified in his discipline of his people. But he also pleads with God for the ultimate deliverance of Israel and the restoration of Jerusalem (9:16–19). In response to this prayer, Daniel is met with yet another vision; the angel Gabriel appears before him with a message. After reminding Daniel that he is greatly loved by God, Gabriel offers yet another glimpse of what is to come for God's people and God's place. These prophetic words from Gabriel, which end Daniel 9, are certainly not easy to understand. While there is the promise of God's final establishment of righteousness for his people in his place (9:24), there are a series of numbers given, as well as a prediction of great suffering and desolation in the place of worship (9:25–27). Ultimately, Gabriel's words hold out the promise of God's eternal reign of peace, which will eventually come through the suffering of the Anointed One and his final sacrifice on the cross, which will put an end to sacrifices and offerings forever!

Read Daniel 9:1–27.

GETTING STARTED

1. What are the biggest barriers to prayer in your life today? Are they time-related (the busyness of life)? Do they have to do with theology (if God is sovereign, why must we pray?)? Discuss the roadblocks to prayer that you face most often.

2. During times of suffering—or times of confusion—how and why might Satan tempt you away from prayer? What practices have been most helpful to you, with regard to prayer, during particularly stressful or trying times?

Daniel's Prayer, pg. 151
It was precisely when Daniel read in the Scriptures . . . that he lifted up his voice in prayer. Daniel didn't turn to prayer because he thought that the prophecy of the seventy years might somehow fail or be delayed if he didn't do so. Rather, it was because he was confident that his sovereign God would do exactly what he had promised to do that he poured out his heart to him in fervent prayer.

OBSERVING THE TEXT

3. What is the context for Daniel's prayer in this chapter? (That is, what has he been reading that leads him to pray in this way?)

4. How would you describe the general shape of Daniel's prayer (9:1–19)? What are the main sections, or parts, to this prayer?

5. How does God respond to Daniel's pleading (9:20–27)? What is hopeful about these verses? What might have brought additional anxiety and restlessness to Daniel, in terms of the timing of God's ultimate restoration?

UNDERSTANDING THE TEXT

6. How does Daniel begin his prayer by giving praise and honor to God (9:3–4)? What titles and descriptions does he attach to the name of God throughout this prayer? What might this teach us about our attitude and demeanor as we approach our God in prayer?

7. As Daniel continues his prayer on behalf of God's people, in what ways does he confess their sin and guilt (9:5–11)? What language does he use to express the fact that they have deserved the punishment and discipline of God? How does he affirm God's justice and righteousness (9:12–15)?

8. What does Daniel ask of God toward the end of his prayer (9:16–19)? How can he be sure that this request is in line with the will of God? With what language and tone does Daniel make his appeal to God?

9. What is comforting and encouraging about the first words of Gabriel to Daniel (9:20–23)? Why does Gabriel say he has come? What does he tell Daniel about the purpose of the words that he will speak to him?

God's Timescale, pg. 167
Daniel 9 shows us that God's timescale for the sanctification of his people and the renovation of the world is far larger than we typically think. He is not as concerned as we are with fixing us right away, nor is he in the business of transforming our friends and family members into perfect saints immediately. To be sure, he will accomplish the complete transformation and sanctification of our lives eventually.

10. What ultimate hope for God's people is promised in 9:24? How should this shape our vision and expectation for God's ultimate purpose for the world—and for his church?

11. What do the final three verses of the chapter (9:25–27) teach Daniel about the timescale of God's final establishment of righteousness? How would you describe the different "stages" of God's restorative work that Gabriel mentions? How does 9:26 point forward to the coming of the Messiah, whose life will be cut off in the process of bringing sacrifices to an end?

BIBLE CONNECTIONS

12. As was mentioned above, it is Daniel's study of God's Word that leads him directly into his earnest prayer on behalf of God's people. While we do not know for sure, Daniel could have been reading Jeremiah 25:11–12. Read those verses now. What do they indicate about the punishment and ultimate restoration of God's people?

13. One way in which Daniel typifies Jesus Christ in this chapter is in his intercessory role. He pleads with God on behalf of a sinful people, making intercession for them before the throne of heaven. Look through the "High Priestly Prayer" of Jesus in John 17. How does Jesus intercede for his people in that prayer? What does he ask of God with regard to his followers?

THEOLOGY CONNECTIONS

14. The reality of the sovereignty of God has often been an excuse for people not to pray. "If God already controls the future," they say, "what difference will my prayers make?" How is this passage a rebuttal to this mind-set? How does the sovereign plan of God impact and shape the prayers of Daniel in this passage?

15. Daniel 9:26–27 points to "an anointed one" who will be cut off—and will also bring an end to sacrifices and offerings. Through Jesus' death on the cross, according to the Westminster Confession of Faith, "Christ, by his obedience and death, did fully discharge the debt of all those that are thus justified, and did make a proper, real, and full satisfaction to his Father's justice in their behalf" (11.3). Given this description of the accomplishment of Jesus on the cross, why does it make sense that he "put an end" to sacrifices and offerings?

APPLYING THE TEXT

16. How ought the prayer of Daniel in the first part of this chapter affect your own prayer life? In what ways have you been challenged to pray for God's people or on behalf of your church?

17. How could you discipline yourself to allow your prayers to be more directly shaped by the truths of God's Word? What truths about Jesus Christ and his gospel might encourage you to pray with more courage, confidence, and power?

18. What can the gradual unfolding of God's restoration of his people (revealed by Gabriel to Daniel) teach you about God's patience, timing, and plan? How can you seek to understand current world events and the apparent slowness of Christ's return more from God's perspective?

Looking for God's Final Reign, pg. 174

Our eyes must constantly be straining forward, looking for the time when the new covenant will be consummated in fullness, when we will drink the cup of the new covenant with the Lord Jesus around that heavenly table. On that day, all of our transgression will be finished, our sin ended, our wickedness atoned for, and our eternal righteousness assured forever. Then, the new Jerusalem will come down from heaven and usher in God's final reign of peace and rest, and we shall reign with him in glory.

PRAYER PROMPT

More than half of this chapter that you have just studied consists of Daniel's prayer to God on behalf of God's people. First, thank God for the greater Daniel—Jesus Christ—who intercedes even now for you at the right hand of the throne of God in heaven! Second, ask God for grace to prayerfully, faithfully, and expectantly wait for his final establishment of righteousness through the reign of his Son. Thank him that the Anointed One has come; beg him for grace to expectantly look for his second coming!

LESSON 11

PREPARED FOR BATTLE

Daniel 10:1–11:1

THE BIG PICTURE

The final three chapters of the book of Daniel make up a unified, final section. Daniel experiences a dramatic concluding vision, which reveals to him the cosmic conflict that exists now—and will continue until the final victory of God. In Daniel 10, we find the prophet continuing in a state of prayer and humility before God (as in chapter 9). In the opening verses, he is forgoing fine foods and lotions in an effort to meditate on God and pray for God's people (10:1–3). Daniel is then suddenly confronted by a stunning angelic figure—clad in military garb, prepped for battle. Daniel is, at first, overcome with fear at this visitation; he essentially faints from fright. Ultimately, though, the angelic visitor delivers his word to Daniel, with another pause in 10:15–19 for Daniel to gather his strength and breath! The heavenly warrior describes his role in battle with the kingdom of Persia and foretells the rise of the kingdom of Greece. He also describes his support for the ascension of Darius the Mede, revealing God's hidden hand in the worldly wars, struggles, and conflicts that continue even today. We learn that the battles of earthly kingdoms point to a cosmic battle, which will one day be finally won by the Savior, King, and very Son of God. God's people continue faithfully to await his return and judgment.

Read Daniel 10:1–11:1.

GETTING STARTED

1. Are there times when you struggle with your ordinary life feeling mundane, unexciting, and monotonous? How do you seek to remind yourself—and those around you—of the eternal significance of every day?

2. Describe some moments or seasons of your life during which you have been especially aware of God's supernatural work behind the scenes. How did you become aware of this?

The Ongoing Conflict, pg. 177

[This chapter] shows us that the conflicts we experience here on earth are the counterpart of a great spiritual conflict that is presently ongoing in the heavenly realm. An awareness of this great spiritual conflict will help us be prepared for the challenges of life here on earth, by being clothed in the appropriate spiritual armor.

OBSERVING THE TEXT

3. In what state of mind and heart do we find Daniel as this chapter begins? How does this connect to the previous chapter we studied? What are we learning about the character of Daniel?

4. How is the angelic visitor described to us? What does the narrator seem to want us to notice about him?

5. What is confusing in this passage? On your first reading of it, what were the main questions that were raised in your mind? Were there any shocking moments or surprises to you as a reader?

UNDERSTANDING THE TEXT

6. What is described for us in the opening verses of this chapter is not a fast, but rather Daniel's intentional restraint in enjoying certain pleasures and fine things for the sake of prayer and mourning for God's people. What seems to be his motivation in this behavior, as the chapter begins?

7. Some commentators suggest that there are two different angelic figures who visit Daniel in this chapter (one speaking in 10:5–6; another lifting him to his feet in 10:10). Why might it be better to understand the text as presenting one angelic figure (see "Bible Connections" below for further discussion)?

8. Look at Daniel's response to the vision (10:7–9). What should this communicate to us about the holiness and glory of God? How is this similar to other reactions that humans have throughout Scripture when confronted with God (or with God's representative)?

9. How are verses 10–11 comforting and encouraging to Daniel? Why should we be encouraged, as God's people today, by these words of God?

Satan's Opposition to the Church, pg. 185

Nor should we suppose that since Persia and Greece are ancient history, these angels are now resting on their laurels. The satanic forces opposed to the church continue to use the powers and institutions of this world in their struggle against God's people. Throughout history, Satan's enmity against the church will be vented time and again.

10. The angel describes his role—behind the scenes—in the political conflicts of Daniel's day (see 10:12–14 and 10:20–21). What does this teach us about the cosmic and heavenly realities that lie behind struggles and wars in our world? Why are these heavenly realities so important for Christians to remember?

11. What do the words of the angel tell us about the hidden hand of God in our world today? What might we learn about the strategies of Satan to influence earthly kingdoms and powers? How does this passage show us the need for the return of Jesus Christ and our need for faith and trust in him?

BIBLE CONNECTIONS

12. There are several similarities between the angelic visitor of Daniel 10 and the angelic beings described by the prophet Ezekiel. Take a moment to read Ezekiel's description of the cherubim (Ezek. 1:1–24); then, read his record of the angelic mediator in Ezekiel 9:2–4. What similarities do you observe between Ezekiel's account and Daniel's vision in Daniel 10? Why might this lead us to identify just one angelic figure in Daniel 10?

13. As Daniel received this vision, some of God's people had been sent back to Jerusalem by Cyrus to begin rebuilding the city. We know from Ezra and Nehemiah that this would have been exciting, but also discouraging, since Jerusalem was in ruins and the returned exiles faced significant opposition. How might this vision have acknowledged the struggle of God's people, but also given them some measure of understanding and hope in God's ways and work?

THEOLOGY CONNECTIONS

14. As you have seen, the awesome holiness of God is a major theme in this chapter of Daniel. John Calvin once wrote about the consistency of the Bible in describing the "dread and amazement with which . . . holy men were struck and overwhelmed" in the presence of God (*Institutes*, 1.1.3). What are some biblical examples of this that you can name? How ought this to shape our view of God?

15. The Westminster Confession of Faith speaks to God's role in the establishment of human governments: "God, the supreme Lord and King of all the world, hath ordained civil magistrates, to be, under him, over the people, for his own glory, and the public good" (23.1). What truth is explained in this phrase? How does Daniel 10 *expand* and further explain this truth?

APPLYING THE TEXT

16. Daniel continues to serve as an example for us in his role as prayerful intercessor for the people of God, even forgoing human comforts as he prays for them. How can we learn from Daniel's commitment to prayer and restraint? How might we apply his example to our prayer for Christians in other parts of the world today?

17. Daniel's first response to the angelic visitor is to faint from fear; he loses his strength and breath again in 10:15–19. How should these responses by Daniel shape our approach to God in prayer? How should they expand our understanding of God's awful holiness and immense glory?

18. How should the angel's description of the cosmic battles, lurking behind earthly conflicts, shape our understanding of our world today? In what ways should this help us pray for our world? How can this passage help us to strengthen our hope in Jesus and our longing for his return?

Assurance of Heavenly Rest, pg. 189
Here is great cause for rejoicing and praise, even during the difficult and frustrating conflicts of life! The decisive battle is already over and God has won the victory. As a result, at the end of our earthly conflict, however fierce that may be, our glorious rest in heaven is firmly assured.

PRAYER PROMPT

We should take note of Daniel's consistent response to God's glorious repre-sentative throughout this chapter: he is filled with fear, reverence, humility, awe, and weakness. A first prayerful response to this chapter should be to acknowledge God's infinite holiness, glory, and power; ask God, now, for a greater grasp of who he is! Then, pray that God would help you understand the cosmic conflict that lurks behind worldly conflicts today—and even the conflicts of your life. Ask him for renewed trust and faith in the one who has won the battle at the cross—and will one day return.

LESSON 12

WARS AND RUMORS OF WARS

Daniel 11:2–12:3

THE BIG PICTURE

As you may know, you have come in your study of Daniel to one of the most difficult and highly disputed sections of the book. In this passage, the angelic figure continues to speak to Daniel, in order to reveal "the truth" to him about the coming rise and fall of the empires of the world (11:2). What follows is a lengthy description of nation after nation, and ruler after ruler, rising to power and being replaced by successors. The angel presents to Daniel, really, a history of the entire world, which focuses in with precision on certain kings and kingdoms, while completely skipping over others. The angel begins by describing the rise of Persia, with its pinnacle coming during the reign of Xerxes (11:2), before it is overtaken by the Greek empire of Alexander the Great (11:3). The Greek kingdom gives way to the competing kingdoms of the final centuries before the coming of Christ, whose events and rulers are described with startling detail by the angel (11:4–20). More detail is then given to the description of the reign and activities of one king—probably Antiochus Epiphanes—who makes war, not only on the nations of the world, but on God's own people as well (11:21–35). As the prophecy continues to ramp up, it seems that Antiochus is still the one being described, although it also seems like a bigger reality comes into view—as if the angel is now speaking of a final king who is much more powerful and evil (11:36–45). Ultimately, the angel Michael rises up against this king and—after a time of intense struggle and suffering—God's people are raised up to eternal life, as the enemies of God are punished and defeated (12:1–3).

Read Daniel 11:2–12:3.

GETTING STARTED

1. What are some of the different views of world history that you have heard or learned? How do historians tend to explain the rise and fall of empires? How ought we to think about history differently as Christians, who believe in a sovereign God?

2. In what ways have you seen the end of the world represented in recent films, books, cartoons, or stories? How do the creators of imaginative end-time narratives factor God into their portrayals (or not)? Why do you think this is the case?

A Selective Overview, pg. 193
The message Daniel received was a prophetic (and very selective) overview of the flow of history from the time of Daniel in the late sixth century B.C. until the end of the world, the final climactic conflict and victory of God.

OBSERVING THE TEXT

3. As you read through this passage, in particular the description of the kings and rulers who rise up, what traits and actions do they have in common? What seems to motivate these powerful rulers of the world?

4. In what ways does this passage ramp up toward the end of chapter 11 and the beginning of chapter 12? What happens just before the final victory for God and his people (12:1)?

5. What is the final hope that concludes this passage? Why is there such good news for God's people in 12:2–3?

UNDERSTANDING THE TEXT

6. This vision came to Daniel during the reign of Cyrus, as many Jews had begun the difficult and dangerous process of returning to Jerusalem and rebuilding the temple and the city walls. They had been ruled by Babylon and Persia, and power would soon pass to the Greeks and then the Romans. How is this historical context helpful in giving us

the big picture of Daniel's vision? Why might this angelic explanation have been good for Daniel's perspective on world events in his day?

7. As the angel begins describing the progression from empire to empire in 11:2–4, what descriptions and predictions sound familiar, based on earlier dreams in the book of Daniel?

8. If you look ahead to the first few verses of Daniel 12, you'll see that this vision given to Daniel is a brief history of the world—from his day to the final judgment. But, it's also a very selective history! As you look through this passage, what particular events or rulers receive special attention? Why do you think this is? What events or rulers seem to be missing? Why might that be?

Putting Trials in Perspective, pg. 200
Why did Daniel need to hear about this history in his situation? The goal was to put the difficulties that the Jews were facing in 536 B.C. in perspective. There was nothing unique about the trials and tribulations that faced them. . . . Their experience should therefore not surprise them, as if something unexpected and out of control were happening to them. God was in control of these machinations as well.

9. How would you describe the events and the changes taking place in Daniel 11:5–20? How many different kings or rulers are named? What happens to them?

10. What seems to characterize the reign of the king who rises up in 11:21–35? What does he do? What seems to motivate him?

11. How do the role and actions (and evil!) of this great king expand and grow from 11:36 to 11:45? In what ways does he wreak havoc on earth? How does he attack God and his people? What is the final hope for God's people (12:1–3), and how should this shape our vision of the future for those who are saved by Jesus Christ?

BIBLE CONNECTIONS

12. Read Paul's strong statement in 1 Corinthians 15:19. What does he mean by that? Why do the descriptions in Daniel 11:2–12:3 make Paul's point even more poignant?

13. As many students of the Bible have observed, this passage in Daniel—especially the final verses—find parallels in the book of Revelation. Read Revelation 17:12–14. What themes in those verses are similar to ones in this passage in Daniel? What hope is held out for God's people?

THEOLOGY CONNECTIONS

14. While this passage in the book of Daniel describes the rise and fall of many kings (and the terrible evil and suffering that their reigns produce), the final word is the resurrection and eternal glory of God's people. The Heidelberg Catechism tells me that, as a Christian: "My flesh, raised by the power of Christ, shall be reunited with my soul and made like Christ's glorious body" (Q&A 57). How do you see this comforting hope described in the opening verses of Daniel 12?

15. As was mentioned earlier, Christians often disagree about the timing of the final judgment and the return of Jesus Christ (as well as the identity and meaning of the "Antichrist" and other matters related to eschatology). What does this passage make clear about the suffering and hardship during the final days before Christ's return (12:1)? What does it teach us about the inevitability of God's victory for his people?

APPLYING THE TEXT

16. What does this passage—and the fact that these predictions come from the mouth of God's angel—tell us about the way we ought to view world history and world events? How should this chapter of Scripture shape our understanding of God's sovereignty, plan, and control of all things?

17. While the bulk of Daniel's vision has to do with kings and kingdoms that are now long past, how should it shape the way we think about our world today? How should this impact our view of politics—and even the way we pray for nations and their rulers?

18. How does this passage comfort you regarding the salvation you have in Jesus Christ? In what ways can and should you think more often about the return of Christ, the final judgment, and the glorious resurrection of the dead in Christ?

PRAYER PROMPT

Daniel 11 confronts us with the rise and fall of empires—magnificently strong in the eyes of the world, but completely subject to the sovereign will of God. As you begin a time of prayer, start by thanking God for his sovereign control over the powers of this world. Ask him to help you remember his complete and total providence. Then, pray that he would help you, by faith, to continue trusting and hoping in Jesus Christ. Ask him for hope in the final resurrection and glorious future for the children of God, who will, in the presence of their Savior, shine "like the stars forever and ever" (12:3).

All of Grace, pg. 208
It is because Christ has suffered and died and has risen again that history has meaning and purpose. It is because Christ has shed his blood for me that I can look forward to spending eternity in his light. Our heavenly inheritance is all of grace, and that glorious prospect will make any sacrifice God calls us to make in this life more than worthwhile.

LESSON 13

HOW LONG WILL I BE BROKEN?

Daniel 12:4–13

THE BIG PICTURE

As we conclude our study in the book of Daniel, we find Daniel's final vision drawing to a close. The historical setting remains unchanged from the previous two chapters; his vision is coming during the return of some of the Jewish exiles to Jerusalem, where they face ongoing suffering, trials, and resistance. The question hanging over the passage (and over Daniel's own heart) is "How long, O Lord?" Daniel is transported in his vision to the edge of a stream of water, where he receives his final messages from two angelic visitors. Daniel is told twice that the words and messages of his visions must be "shut up" and "sealed" until the appointed time (12:4, 9). He is reminded that all that he has seen and heard will indeed come to pass; times of trial and tribulation will come, and God's final judgment and salvation will be ultimately revealed. But much time will pass; several different numbers are given to Daniel, which represent the passage of time through tribulation up until the end. The passage ends with one final word of confirmation, hope, and assurance for Daniel: at the end of days, he will "stand" firmly, for he has been faithful (12:13). Chapter 12, then, concludes Daniel's apocalyptic vision—as well as the entire book—with a message of ultimate hope for God's people. Much time will pass, along with many trials and troubles for God's people. Yet hope for ultimate restoration, salvation, and even resurrection remains for those who humbly put their faith in the Savior.

Read Daniel 12:4–13.

GETTING STARTED

1. What are some examples of our culture's obsession with instant gratification that you regularly observe? How can a desire for immediate comfort and healing collide with a biblical call for patience—especially as we wait for the return of Jesus Christ and the perfect, final justice of God?

2. Given all that Daniel has seen and heard up to this point in the book, what questions might he want to ask God at this point? What are some questions that *you* sometimes want to ask God about his ways, his timing, or the events that will lead to the return of Jesus Christ?

Addressing Hard Questions, pg. 212

The Book of Daniel never assumes that we would find living in a world like this easy. On the contrary, it anticipates the fact that we will frequently find ourselves crying out: "How long, O Lord? Where are you? What are you doing? Why are your people dying and despairing? Why are they not prospering and victorious? How long do you think that we can hold on?" These are the questions that Daniel 12 is designed to address.

OBSERVING THE TEXT

3. What is confusing or puzzling to you in this passage? What is your first reaction to the time-related descriptions and predictions that the angelic messengers give to Daniel? Have you heard various interpretations of these times and numbers?

4. What specific questions are asked in these verses (by the angelic messenger and by Daniel)? How are they answered? What remains mysterious—or not fully answered?

5. How is Daniel's character affirmed throughout this passage? What words of hope and encouragement are given to him in these verses?

UNDERSTANDING THE TEXT

6. What might it mean that the words and visions that Daniel is receiving (and has received) must be "shut up" until the end (12:4, 9)? Why is

this important for us to understand? How does this point to the mystery of God's will and the hiddenness of his plan?

7. As you have already observed, this passage is shaped by two questions about the end of time and the judgment of God (see 12:6, 8). What do these questions seek to discover? How are they answered? What truths are clear, and what remains mysterious?

8. What does the angel's question (12:6) imply about the heavenly audience to the cosmic battle currently being waged? How might the suffering and faithfulness of Christians in this world encourage and teach even the angels in heaven?

The Need for Perseverance, pg. 216

Taken together, then, these numbers [in 12:7 and 12:11] characterize history as a whole as a time of judgment and trial. At the same time, they remind us that this time of trial is limited by the Lord's mercy, that its precise end is known to the Lord though utterly impenetrable by human logic, and that we need to persevere in faith until the very end.

9. In answer to the "how long?" questions in this passage, both of the times given in Daniel's vision are about three and a half years in length (12:7, 11). What does the length of this time imply about the trials and tribulations of our world? In what ways does the brevity of the time point to God's mercy and the ultimate restoration of righteousness?

10. Daniel is told that the end will finally come "when the shattering of the power of the holy people comes to an end" (12:7). Why is this surprising? What might this mean? How might this point to God's victory through suffering, and his strength being revealed through weakness? How are these ironies perfectly revealed through the Holy One and his suffering on the cross?

11. How would Daniel have heard the words of 12:13 as a wonderful encouragement? How should those words encourage and strengthen us, as followers of Jesus today? In what ways did the opening verses of this chapter (12:1-3) fill out a vision of the final hope for God's people after suffering and trial?

BIBLE CONNECTIONS

12. Take a moment to read Isaiah 65:17–19—words of prophecy that Daniel and God's people would have known well. Why might God's people have doubted his fulfillment of this promise in their current situation? How do Daniel's visions in chapters 10–12 further explain how and when God will fulfill the words of Isaiah?

13. Read Revelation 19:11–16—a glorious vision of the final victory of the Lord Jesus Christ. How must this passage shape our hope as followers of Jesus? What descriptions of Jesus—his person and his work—are most encouraging to you as you read that prediction of his glorious coming?

THEOLOGY CONNECTIONS

14. Daniel 12 wonderfully illustrates what is sometimes called the *perspicuity*, or *clarity*, of Scripture. Scripture's perspicuity refers to its clarity regarding the fundamental and core teachings of the faith. While one can debate the meaning of the time periods mentioned in this chapter, what fundamental teachings are clearly affirmed in Daniel 12?

15. The Scottish Reformer John Knox is said to have once exclaimed, "A man with God is always in the majority."[1] How might Daniel's vision in this chapter have affirmed this truth in his heart, despite the appearance of massive worldly resistance, power, and persecution aimed against God's people?

APPLYING THE TEXT

16. One truth that permeates the book of Daniel—and especially these final ten verses—is the fact of our world's utter brokenness. Because of sin and depravity, our world cannot be fixed; it needs to be entirely redeemed and re-created by Jesus the King. How ought this reality to shape our prayer life? Our expectations? Our approach to politics? Our ultimate hope?

17. How should the truths of this passage in Daniel shape our understanding of our suffering and brokenness? Why should the brokenness of Jesus on the cross help us understand the role of suffering in the lives of Christians?

1. Inscribed on the Reformation Wall in Geneva, Switzerland.

18. In what ways does this chapter help us to better understand the current state of our world? How does Daniel's vision expand our expectations for the renewal and redemption that only God himself can bring to our world?

PRAYER PROMPT

As we close our study of the book of Daniel, we ought to end with a renewed sense of biblical *realism* as we look at our world. Sin and evil are very real, and trouble will increase until Jesus returns. Yet we also end with great *hope*. Daniel's visions point us to God's ultimate victory and judgment; the salvation of his people is secure through his Son, who was broken for us and was raised gloriously to life again. Praise God today for the glorious hope that Christians have in Jesus, the crucified, risen, and returning King!

Our Task as Martyrs, pg. 223

The day is coming when Jesus Christ will ride out to conquer and to re-create, a day when the kingdom of this world will become the kingdom of our God and of his Christ (Rev. 11:15). In the meantime, our task as martyrs is simply to testify to the Lord's greatness and grace by our words and by our sufferings. As we cling to God in the midst of trials that we do not understand, we testify of God's grace to a watching world and to the heavenly beings.

Jon Nielson is senior pastor of Spring Valley Presbyterian Church in Roselle, Illinois, and the author of *Bible Study: A Student's Guide*, among other books. He has served in pastoral positions at Holy Trinity Church, Chicago, and College Church, Wheaton, Illinois, and as director of training for the Charles Simeon Trust.

Iain M. Duguid (PhD, University of Cambridge) is professor of Old Testament at Westminster Theological Seminary in Philadelphia. He has written numerous works of biblical exposition, including *Daniel* in the Reformed Expository Commentary series, *Ezekiel* in the NIV Application Commentary series, and *Numbers* in the Preaching the Word series.